Omani Kitty's Journey of Colors

Written and Illustrated by Kathy Griffith

A friendly kitten named Omani Kitty is proud of her beautiful shades of red, yellow, white, and black. Little did she know, big changes in her life were about to take place in a journey of colors.

Omani Kitty, her mama, and brother Takota have moved to a new neighborhood of green and purple cats. Omani is sad when she finds out that her neighbors do not like cats who are red, yellow, white, and black.

3

Welcome

Omani watches the kitties throw and catch balls in new ways that she has never seen. When she gets enough courage to say "Hi", they ignore her as if she is invisible.
"It's true, what I heard, that kitties here don't like my colors," she whispers.
Omani quietly leaves, but she doesn't give up. She thinks and thinks.
"Yes, I got it!" she exclaims.

Back home Omani paints her colors green and purple with stripes and circles just like the other kitties.
"I can't wait to show the neighbors my new colors, but now I need to practice playing like them," she says.

Omani tries, but she is having more fun catching, throwing, and spinning the balls in her own way.
Omani dodges the balls as she dashes out the door.
She is exhausted and done playing for the day.

She curls up in her soft bed.
Slowly, her eyes close and she drifts into a deep sleep.
She has a colorful dream.

8

A wise hawk swoops down and gently carries Omani away.
Through the meadows, over the river, and into the valley far away
from home.

The wise hawk takes her to a special
tree in the land of the birds.
"What should I do?" Omani asks, as she is about
to begin an incredible journey.

"Look for the signs and the many birds will guide you through," the wise hawk replies.
Omani Kitty jumps down from the tree. She waits and watches.

Finally, three cheerful storks appear.
"We are Kaysa, Kyan and Anpo," the storks say. "We will gladly take you to Lollipop Hill. Perhaps the signs there are the ones you seek."

Among the wild lollipops Omani sees a line of
red, yellow, white, and black signs.
She stops and reads,
"Be strong in your heart."

"Could this be a sign for me? Because my true colors are also red, yellow, white, and black," she wonders. The sun sets and the time has come for the storks to prepare Omani for her journey back home.

The storks have a great idea. They pick, sort, and arrange their feathers.

Together, they make Omani Kitty the most beautiful wings she has ever seen.

She dances in delight. She swirls around and swings her green
and purple wings.

Omani Kitty has learned from the storks how to fly.
She is ready to leave and waves goodbye.

The storks shout out to Omani, "Stop at the giant red and green branches. The birds there will guide you in the right direction."

When she arrives, she is surprised to meet all types of colorful birds.
After spending time with her new friends, Omani Kitty realizes that she could be any size, any shape, any color and that no matter how she looks they will still love her.

Omani Kitty and the birds fly together, united through diversity.
She is excited about her new adventure.

19

Suddenly, they meet a fierce storm.
They fly down to take shelter in a corn field.
"Oh no!" Omani says, when she sees that a little bit of
her colors have washed away.

"It doesn't matter to the birds, but what about my new neighbors, the green and purple kitties?" she mutters.

The birds fly back out of the corn field to the lovely sky.
Jayla Blue Jay stays with Omani.
"I lost my way!" Omani cries to Jayla Blue Jay.

22

"Be strong in your heart and you will be okay," Jayla kindly says. Jace the Owl wants to help her too. "Believe in yourself and you will find your way," he explains.

Jayla Blue Jay and Jace the Owl guide Omani Kitty out of the valley, over the river and across the meadows, on the rest of her journey back home. She can't wait to see her family.

Omani made it to the end of her journey of colors. She dances, she swirls and swings. She hangs up her beautiful precious wings. "I found my way!" she sighs.

Omani's dream comes to an end as the rain washes away her green and purple blend.

She looks up to the sky and shouts out, "Thank you wise Hawk, Jayla Blue Jay, Jace the Owl and all the birds for taking me on this journey of colors. I love my red, yellow, white and black colors! I am happy now just to be me."

Omani Kitty discovers what really matters.
Her family and friends who love her just as she is.

Omani's story doesn't end yet.
She wants children to come together and join her in bringing unity through diversity to people of all colors.

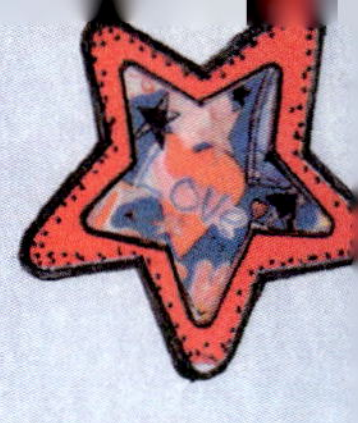

Omani Kitty's colorful journey continues with you.
You are beautiful just as you are.
Believe in yourself and be strong in your heart!

Your Picture and Name

Dedicated to Blaine Pourier
and all of our children
who made their final journey to the spirit world.
Lost but not forgotten, they are with us forever.
Inspired by my beautiful granddaughter
Jayla Rodriguez,
whose life ended when she was just 8 years old.
Proud to be Native American,
she had a special place in her heart for all people.
A little piece of Jayla's artwork is on each page.

"Be strong in your heart die

or not die it is all about life." (Jayla 2013)

The Author/Illustrator

Kathy Griffith is an enrolled member of the Oglala Sioux Tribe. She grew up with her parents and six siblings on and around the Pine Ridge Indian Reservation in South Dakota. Her maternal and paternal ancestry began in the early 1800's with her 3rd great-grandparents, four strong Native American women and their white fur trapper/trader husbands. Their history reveals that they had a compatible existence. However, the next generations experienced 200 years of tragedy and destruction ending in a loss of land, freedom and life.

Kathy has a master's degree in Counseling and an associate degree in Commercial Art. She has worked as a Licensed Professional Counselor both on the reservation and off. She believes that Native Americans are healing from historical trauma and beginning to stand together as a united front in causes that impact Native Americans and all people. Her desire is for our entire nation to come together in unity through diversity.

Acknowledgements

I would like to thank the family and friends who have been an encouragement throughout the writing and illustration process of this book, especially my mom, Mary McGaa. Special mention goes to Cami Griffith, Danielle Griffith, Jan Sheats, Linda Hogan, Adryan Short, and Doyle McGaa.

Published and printed in the United States
ISBN 978-1-56492-523-7